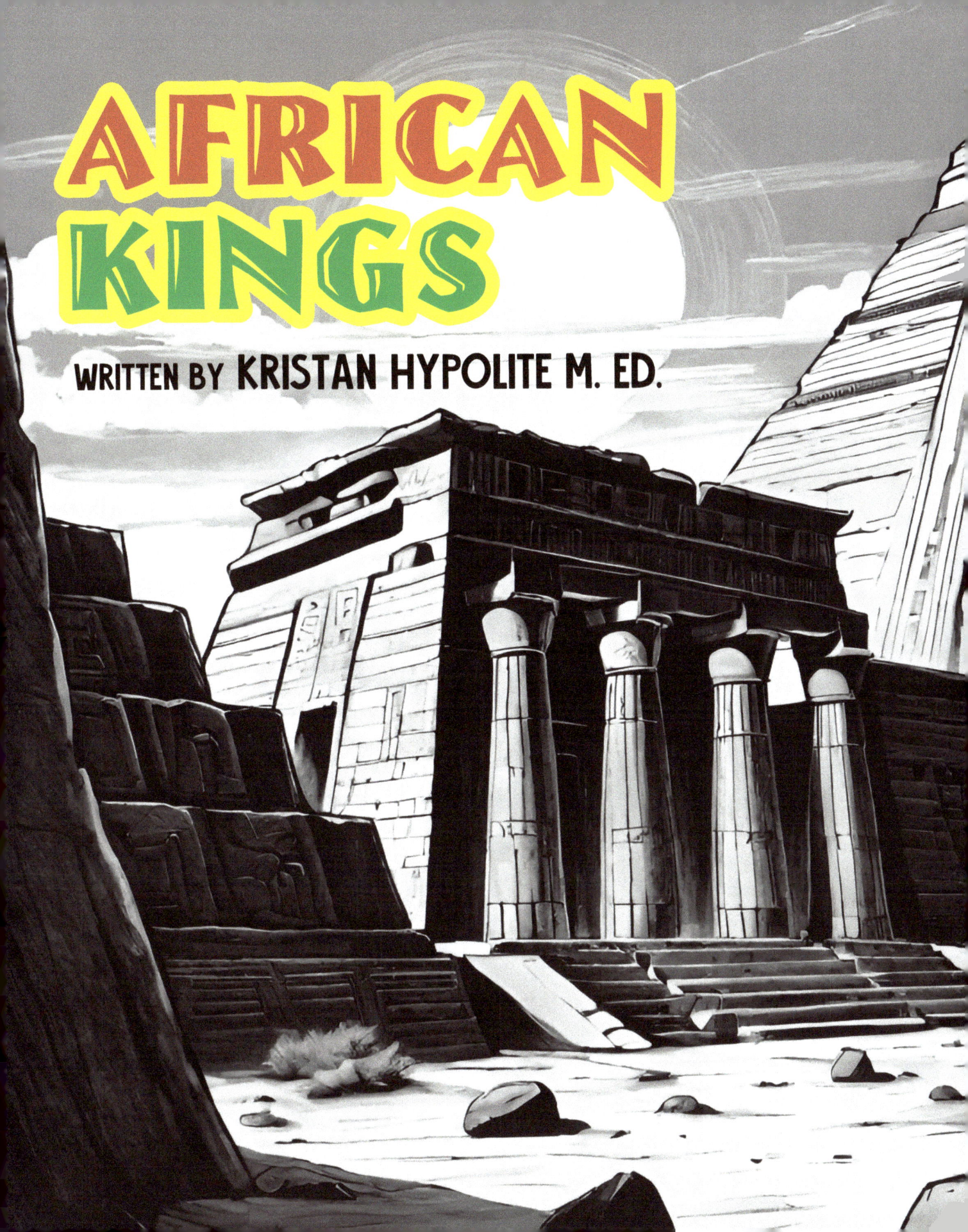

Copyright © 2025
Written by Kristan Hypolite M. Ed.

ISBN#: 979-8-9912063-5-8

All rights reserved. No part of this book may be reproduced in any form without permission from the author or publisher, except as permitted by U.S. copyright law.

Illustrations Copyright © Kristan Hypolite M. Ed.

Book Design and Illustrations by by Uzuri Designs
www.uzuridesignsbooks.com
bookdesigner@uzuridesignsbooks.com

AFRICAN KINGS

WRITTEN BY KRISTAN HYPOLITE M. ED.

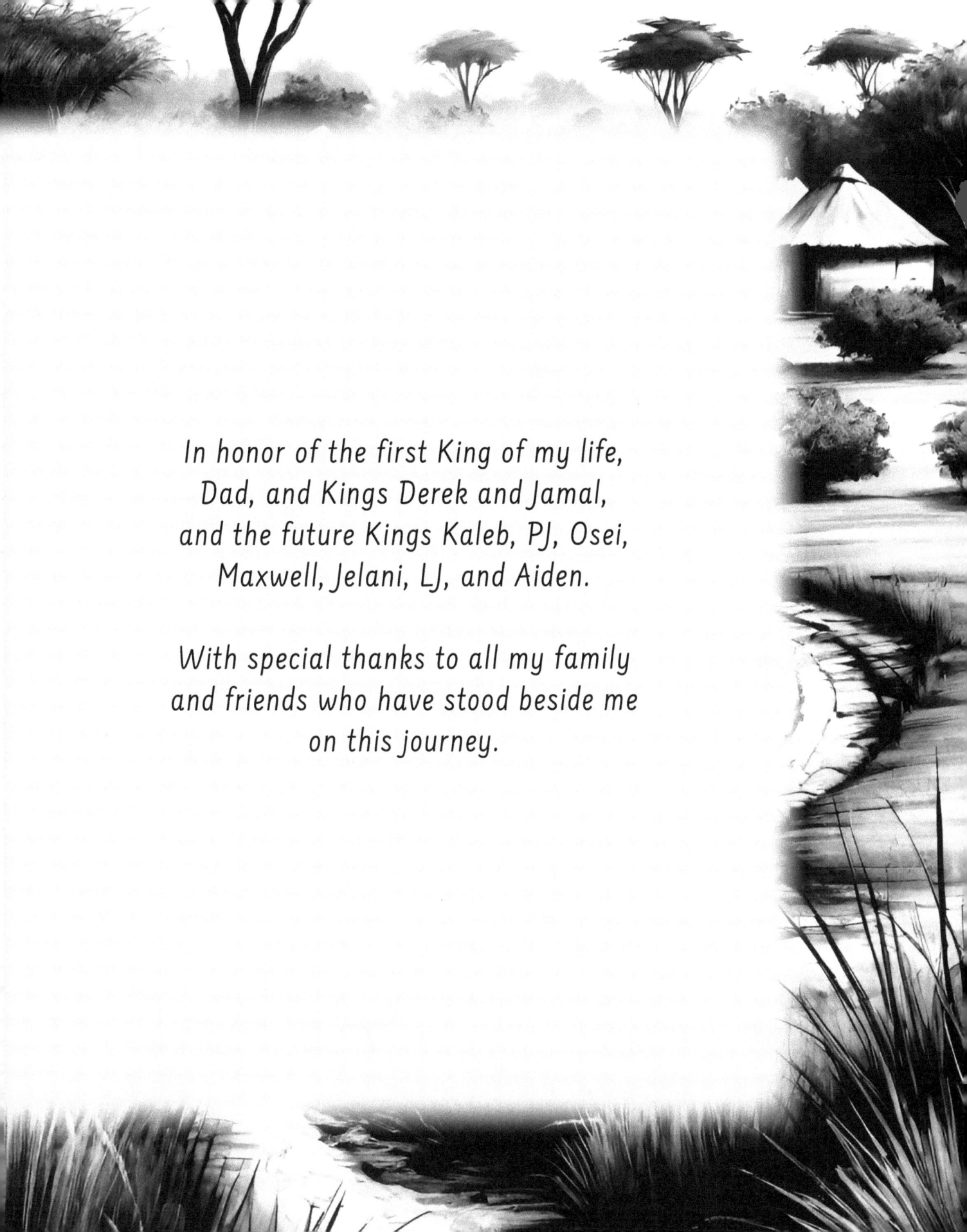

In honor of the first King of my life,
Dad, and Kings Derek and Jamal,
and the future Kings Kaleb, PJ, Osei,
Maxwell, Jelani, LJ, and Aiden.

With special thanks to all my family
and friends who have stood beside me
on this journey.

PREFACE

As Kaleb turned three, life was filled with mystery. It all started when Kaleb explored grandma's living room and discovered a collage of family photos. Kaleb would always ask questions about family, where they lived, what their lives were like and what happened to them. I would often ask those same questions about our history.

His thirst for knowledge only grew stronger which ignited my passion about our history. Together delving into albums, books and documentaries, we continued to uncover mysteries of life past and present with our curiosity as our guiding light.

I admire historical figures like Mansa Musa, Frederick Douglas, Carter G. Woodson, and Marcus Garvey for their contributions to society and commitment to advancing social change. Their stories inspire me to strive for greatness in everything that I do.

I believe exploring cultures and customs around the world expands our knowledge of our past to help us navigate our present and shape our future.

TABLE OF CONTENTS

PREFACE	VI
MANSA ABUBAKARI II	1
PHARAOH AKHENATEN	2
PHARAOH AMENHOTEP I	3
KING BEHANZIN	4
KING CETSHWAYO	5
PHARAOH DJER	7
KING ENDUBIS	8
KING GHEZO	9
KING IMHOTEP	10
EMPEROR HAILE SELASSIE I	11
GENERAL HANNIBAL	13
PHARAOH HOREMHEB	15
KING JAJA	17
KING KALEB	19
PHARAOH KHUFU	21
KING LALIBELA	22
PRESIDENT NELSON MANDELA	23
MANSA MUSA	25
ASKIA MUHAMMAD	28
EMPEROR MENELIK I	29
KING NARMER	30

KING PIYE	31
KING QA'A	32
PTAH	33
PHARAOH RAMESSES II	35
EMPEROR SEPTIMIUS SEVERUS	37
PHARAOH NEFERKARE SHABAKA	39
KING SHAKA ZULU	41
KING SOLOMON	43
PHARAOH TAHARQA	45
KABAKA TTEMBO	47
KING TUTANKHAMUN	49
KING USERKRAF	51
ABOUT THE AUTHOR	55
ABOUT THE BOOK	56
REFERENCES	57

MANSA ABUBAKARI II

Mansa Abubakari II was the ruler of the seas from Senegambia, later called Mali Empire, now modern-day Mali. Abubakari sailed across the Atlantic Ocean, marking one of the earliest transatlantic voyages in history.

In 1312 AD, Abubakari traveled to the Americas, which was 180 years before Christopher Columbus. The two primary currents in the Atlantic Ocean, the Canary Current and the Guinea Current, carried Abubakari's ships from West Africa to the Americas.

Abubakari's fleet of 1,000 ships were designed by sailors, shipbuilders, doctors, and stocked with food, water, medicines, and fruits for a two-year voyage.

Abubakari and the Malians who reached the Americas left a lasting legacy by renaming places in honor of themselves. In Haiti, Mandinga Bay, Sierra de Mali, and Mandinga Poet, reflect the influence of the Mali Empire. This fascinating chapter in history highlights the advanced maritime capabilities of African civilizations.

PHARAOH AKHENATEN

Pharaoh Akhenaten was the tenth Pharaoh of the Eighteenth Dynasty of Ancient Egypt from 1351 BCE to 1334 BCE, now modern-day Egypt. Akhenaten was known as "Akhenaten the Great."

Egypt became the most powerful and influential civilization in the world. Akhenaten was born as Amenhotep IV, the younger son of Pharaoh Amenhotep III also known as "Amenhotep the Great." After a 36-year reign, Amenhotep III died and was succeeded by his son, Amenhotep IV, who later changed his name to Akhenaten.

As Pharaoh, Akhenaten shifted Egypt's religious focus from its traditional polytheism to Atenism, the worship of Aten, a sun god. The Hymn to Aten emphasizes Aten's role as the creator of the world, vividly portraying the sun disk as the source of all life. Its rising brings renewal to the earth, while its setting brings rest to all living beings. Several passages parallel literary traditions, particularly those found in Psalm 104.

However, after Akhenaten's death, his religious reforms were abandoned. His monuments and statues were destroyed, and his name was erased from official records. The traditional polytheistic religion of Egypt was restored during the reign of his successor, Tutankhamun.

Akhenaten was married to Queen Nefertiti, who held the title of "Great Royal Wife" and played a significant role in the religious and political affairs of his reign.

PHARAOH AMENHOTEP I

Pharaoh Amenhotep I was the second Pharaoh of the Eighteenth Dynasty of Ancient Egypt from 1526 BCE to 1506 BCE, now modern-day Egypt. Amenhotep I introduced the water clock and funerary texts shaping Egyptian burial traditions.

A significant innovation during Amenhotep I's reign was the development of the first water clock, known as the clepsydra. Unlike modern clocks, hours were not fixed in length. Instead, the clepsydra divided the night into 12 equal segments, which varied with the seasons. This meant that during shorter summer nights, the clock automatically adjusted to measure the shorter hours precisely for both daily life and religious rituals.

Amenhotep I's reign marked significant literary achievements, including the Book of What Is in the Underworld (commonly known as the Egyptian Book of the Dead). His work became a cornerstone of New Kingdom burial practices.

KING BEHANZIN

King Behanzin Gbehanzin was the eleventh King of the Dahomey Kingdom from 1890 to 10 December 1894, now modern-day Benin. Just as the shark fiercely protects the coast, Behanzin was seen as the protector of the Dahomey Kingdom.

Dahomey's army was the most powerful and well-organized in West Africa, consisting of both men and women, including the feared and elite female warriors known as the Dahomey Amazons. One notable Amazon leader, Seh-Dong Hong-Beh, meaning "God speaks true," led a force of 6,000 Dahomey Amazons in an assault on the Egba fortress at Abeokuta, Nigeria in 1851.

The large wooden statue that represents a powerful metaphor for King Behanzin, was displayed in the royal palace of Abomey, and now housed in the Musée Quai Branly in Paris, France.

DAHOMEY KINGDOM

KING CETSHWAYO

King Cetshwayo kaMpande was King of the Zulu Kingdom from 1873 to 1884, now modern-day South Africa. Cetshwayo led the Zulu army and enhanced Shaka Zulu's warfare tactics.

Cetshwayo was the Commander-in-Chief of the Zulu military during the Anglo-Zulu War of 1879. He strengthened the Zulu military by expanding and restoring King Shaka Zulu's military strategies. Cetshwayo established a new capital for the Zulu nation, Ulundi, meaning "The High Place." Also, he expelled European missionaries from the Zulu territory and encouraged other African groups to resist Boer dominance in the Transvaal territory.

His legacy continues today through his son, Dinuzulu, who was crowned king on 20 May 1884. A blue plaque commemorates Cetshwayo at 18 Melbury Road, Kensington, London, England. In 2016, King Cetshwayo District Municipality in South Africa was named in his honor.

ZULU KINGDOM

PHARAOH DJER

Pharaoh Djer was the third Pharaoh of the First Dynasty of Ancient Egypt about 3000 BCE, now modern-day Egypt.

The Palermo Stone, an Ancient Egyptian artifact, noted Djer reigned "41 complete and partial years." Ancient records, often inscribed on stone, clay tablets, or papyrus, served as record-keeping tools for documenting events, laws, and stories.

Djer was the son of Pharaoh Hor-Aha, grandson of Narmer, and husband of Khenthap. Merneith was the daughter of Djer, the wife of King Djet and the mother of King Den. Women with titles later associated with queens, such as "Great One of the Hetes-Sceptre" and "She who Sees/Carries Horus," were buried near Djer's tomb in Abydos, Egypt.

KING ENDUBIS

King Endubis was King of the Kingdom of Axum from 295 AD to 310 AD, now modern-day Ethiopia. Endubis was the first to mint coins.

Endubis set a powerful precedent in the Kingdom of Axum by introducing a standardized system of currency. His coin design became a model for future rulers, featuring a profile bust of the king facing right on both sides. The coins had the inscription "ΑΞΩΜΙΤΩ ΒΑCΙΛΕΥC," meaning "King of Axum," asserting both his royal authority and the growing significance of the Axumite Kingdom.

Endubis introduced currency not only to streamline trade but also to standardize government taxation and the collection of other payments. This innovation contributed to a period of significant economic growth in Axum. The coins were minted in gold, silver, and bronze. While distinctly Axumite in origin, they followed Roman weight standards and used Greek inscriptions, enabling Axsum to actively engage in Greco-Roman trade networks along the Red Sea.

By the 4th century CE, during the reign of King Ezana, Axum had embraced Christianity and aligned itself with the Orthodox tradition. Ezana became the first ruler in history to use the cross of Christ on his coins, replacing earlier crescent symbols. This marked not only a religious transformation but also a strategic use of coinage as a tool of political messaging demonstrating Axum's wealth, spiritual identity, and global connections.

AXUM KINGDOM

KING GHEZO

King Ghezo was King of the Dahomey Kingdom from 1818 to 1858, now modern-day Benin. Ghezo faced external and internal threats by the British blockade of Dahomey's ports aimed at halting the Atlantic slave trade.

His elite female bodyguard unit, known as the Dahomey Amazons, was called the "Mino." Ghezo raised the status of female guards by providing uniforms, advanced weaponry, and innovative military tactics.

The Mino's presence and influence were a testament to Ghezo's strategic vision and recognition of both men and women's roles in the military.

KING IMHOTEP

King Imhotep was an architect, physician, priest, and the third King of the Third Dynasty of Ancient Egypt from 2592 BCE to 2566 BCE, now modern-day Egypt.

Imhotep (Ancient Egyptian: ii-m-ḥtp), meaning "the one who comes in peace," served as chancellor to Pharaoh Djoser and was the architect of the Step Pyramid at Saqqara, one of history's earliest monumental stone structures.

He was the high priest of Ra, the sun god, at Heliopolis, one of the most important religious centers of Ancient Egypt. Imhotep held the title "The King of Lower Egypt, the Two Brothers," which suggest that Imhotep was the twin brother of Pharaoh Djoser.

In the Ptolemaic era, 305 BCE to 30 BCE, Imhotep was the physician and "the god of medicine". The Greeks admired Imhotep's medical knowledge and compared him to Asclepius, a mortal who became their god of healing. The Rod of Asclepius—a snake-entwined staff, similar to the caduceus, remains a symbol of medicine to this day.

Imhotep's legacy as a healer was reflected in the Upper Egyptian Famine Stela for ending a seven-year famine crisis. Today, Imhotep was the main character in the original 1932 film The Mummy and its 2001 sequel The Mummy Returns. Imhotep's legacy remains a symbol of ingenuity, healing, and divine wisdom, and his achievements continue to be celebrated in Egyptian history and across the world.

ANCIENT EGYPT

EMPEROR HAILE SELASSIE I

Emperor Haile Selassie I was Emperor of the Ethiopian Empire from 1930 to 1974, now modern-day Ethiopia. Selassie was an emperor who promoted education and Pan-African unity.

Haile Selassie I (Ge'ez: ቀዳማዊ ኃይለ ሥላሴ, Amharic: [kʼədäˈmäwi ˈhäjlə sɨlˈläse]) was born Tafari Makonnen 23 July 1893 and rose to power as the Enderase (Regent Plenipotentiary) of Ethiopia under Empress Zewditu from 1916 to 1930.

Selassie held divine status within the Rastafari movement, an Abrahamic faith that emerged in the 1930's. He belonged to the Solomonic Dynasty, which traces its origins to Emperor Yekuno Amlak in 1270 AD descendant of Menelik I, the legendary son of King Solomon of the Kingdom of Israel and Queen Makeda of the Kingdom of Sheba.

In 1931, Selassie introduced Ethiopia's first written constitution. In 1942, he formally abolished slavery and played a pivotal role in Ethiopia's admission to the United Nations.

In 1963, during a visit to the United States amid the Civil Rights Movement, Haile Selassie condemned racial discrimination and advocated for Pan-African unity. That same year, he presided over the founding of the Organisation of African Unity (OAU), the precursor to the African Union, and served as its first chairman. African leaders such as Kwame Nkrumah envisioned the creation of a "United States of Africa."

Selassie's reign ended in 1974, and he was secretly assassinated by the Derg at the Jubilee Palace in Addis Ababa, Ethoipia on August 27, 1975. His remains were buried at the Holy Trinity Cathedral in Addis Ababa, Ethiopia on November 5, 2000.

Selassie played a pivotal role in advancing education and promoting Pan-African unity. He founded Addis Ababa University and Organisation of African Unity, now called the African Union.

His legacy as a prominent anti-colonial leader continues to influence African politics. A 2021 documentary, produced by his granddaughter, explored the history of the Ethiopian royal family. In 2024, Selassie was portrayed in a biographical film that examined his significance in both Ethiopian history and Rastafarian religious tradition.

ETHIOPIAN EMPIRE

GENERAL HANNIBAL

General Hannibal Barca was the greatest African military general of Carthage from 218 BCE to 196 BCE, now modern-day Tunisia.

In 247 BCE, Hannibal Barca was born Chenu Bechola Barca. The Barca family, descendants of Queen Dido-Elissar and renowned for their military prowess, was the origin of the city Barcelona, Spain.

General Hamilcar Barca, Hannibal's father, fought and won back the north-east of Spain from Rome, and made his son Hannibal promise to one day defeat Rome and exterminate the European empire.

Hannibal set out for Italy from Africa with an army of 15,000 men, including 13,000 African and Iberian soldiers. He conquered the tribe of Gaul and many hostile tribes one after another. Hannibal advanced toward the Franco-Italian border near the Pyrenees mountains. Despite severe conditions and the loss of 7,000 men, Hannibal led the remaining forces across the Pyrenees Mountains and crossed the Rhône River with elephants from India and Africa.

Today, Hannibal's legacy of strategic genius and daring tactics continue to be studied in military schools around the world.

PHARAOH HOREMHEB

Pharaoh Horemheb was the last Pharaoh of the Eighteenth Dynasty of Ancient Egypt from 1319 BCE to 1292 BCE, now modern-day Egypt.

Horemheb, whose name means "Horus is in Jubilation," served as Commander-in-Chief of the army under Kings Tutankhamun and Ay before ruling Egypt for 14 years.

Horemheb restored order to Egypt, after Akhenaten's reign had shifted power from the traditional priesthood of Amun to government officials. He appointed judges, regional officials, and reintroduced local religious authorities. Horemheb divided legal authority between Upper and Lower Egypt, by assigning the Viziers of Thebes and Memphis to govern these regions, respectively.

Horemheb was a prolific builder and constructed several monumental structures, including the Second, Ninth, and Tenth

Pylons of the Great Hypostyle Hall at the Temple of Karnak. His reforms are documented at the base of his Tenth Pylon. The Great Edict of Horemheb, contains the king's decree to restore order to the Two Lands and implement domestic reforms.

Horemheb had no surviving sons and appointed his Vizier, Paramessu, as his successor. Paramessu would ascend to the throne as Ramesses I, marking the beginning of the Nineteenth Dynasty. Horemheb reintroduced the ancient religious cults, especially that of Amun, solidifying his role as a true Pharaoh who restored Ma'at, the divine order of the world.

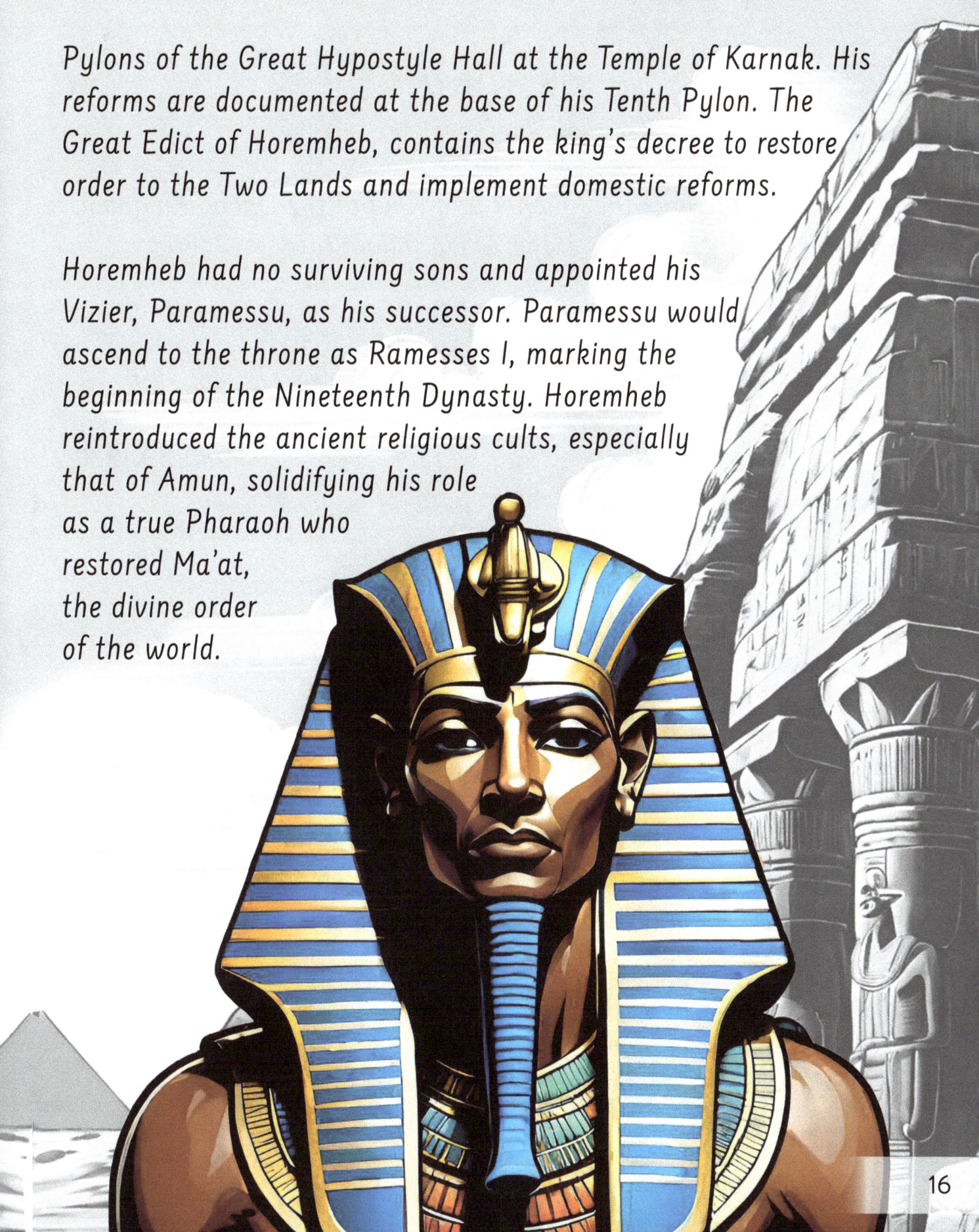

KING JAJA

King Jaja of Opobo was the founder and King of the Opobo Kingdom, now modern-day Rivers State and Akwa Ibom State of Nigeria.

Opobo emerged as a key trading hub in the palm oil industry. King Jaja strategically established a monopoly by excluding both European and African middlemen, instead selling large quantities of palm oil directly to British merchants in Liverpool, England. By 1870, he was exporting over 8,000 tons of palm oil annually.

Despite this commercial rivalry with the Europeans, Jaja was forward-thinking and sent his children to schools in Glasgow, Scotland, established a secular school in Opobo Kingdom, and ensured that no missionaries were allowed to enter his kingdom.

At the 1884 Berlin Conference, European powers designated Opobo as part of British territory. When King Jaja continued to levy taxes on British traders, British authorities arrested him. He was tried in Accra, Ghana, exiled to London, then Saint Vincent, and finally to Barbados in the British West Indies. While in exile, Jaja's presence in Barbados sparked civil unrest and public outrage over the mistreatment of a native African king. In 1891, he was granted permission to return to Opobo, but he died before he could make the journey.

KING KALEB

King Kaleb was King of the Kingdom of Axum, now modern-day Ethiopia.

Kaleb (Ge'ez: ካሌብ, Latin: Caleb), also known as Saint Elesbaan, was named after the biblical figure Caleb. According to Ethiopian tradition, he offered his crown to the Church of the Holy Sepulchre in Jerusalem.

Inscriptions and coins discovered in Axum refer to him as the son of Tazena. Though originally from Lasta, his royal center was in Bugna, at a site later associated with Gebre Mesqel Lalibela.

King Kaleb's legacy lived on through his son, Gebre Mesqel (Ge'ez: ገብረ መስቀል), who succeeded him after Kaleb withdrew from public life to live in a monastery.

Today, Kaleb and his family have two structures in Ethiopia. One is believed to be his tomb, and the other is thought to be that of his son, Gebre Mesqel. Some traditions mention a second son, King Israel of Axum, described as Gebre Mesqel's identical twin.

PHARAOH KHUFU

Pharaoh Khufu was the second Pharaoh of the Fourth Dynasty in the Old Kingdom of Ancient Egypt from 2589 BCE to 2566 BCE, now modern-day Egypt. Khufu built the Great Pyramid of Giza, one of the Seven Wonders of the World.

The Great Pyramid of Giza's base measures 750 x 750 feet (230.4 x 230.4 meters) and stands at a height of 455.2 feet (138.7 meters). Originally, the pyramid stood 481 feet (147 meters) tall, but the pyramidion and much of the limestone casing were lost due to stone robbery. The pyramidion was covered in electrum, and the interior walls and ceilings were made of polished granite. Pharaoh Khufu built the pyramid on a high point of the Giza Plateau to maximize its visibility, naming it Akhet-Khufu, meaning "Horizon of Khufu."

The Great Sphinx of Giza, was part of Khufu's funerary complex. The Sphinx, carved directly from the Giza plateau, measures 241 feet by 66.6 feet (73.5 meters by 20.3 meters) and features the body of a lion with the head of a man, wearing the royal Nemes headdress. Originally, the statue was brightly painted in red, ochre, green, and black.

In 1903, archaeologists found a small ivory figurine in a temple ruin at Abydos, Egypt, believed to be the only known depiction of Pharaoh Khufu.

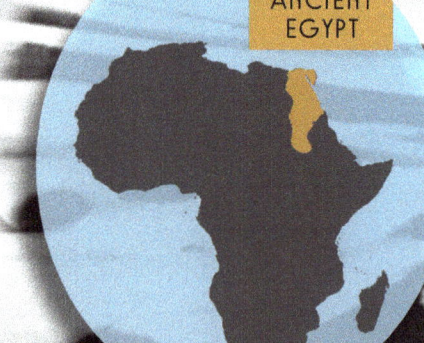
ANCIENT EGYPT

KING LALIBELA

King Lalibela was a Saint and King of the Zagwe Dynasty of the Ethiopian Empire from 1181 AD to 1221 AD, now modern-day Ethiopia.

King Lalibela (Ge'ez: ላሊበላ), was the most famous of the Zagwe monarchs and created eleven iconic monolithic rock-hewn churches of Lalibela carved out of stone with the help of angels. He was later recognized as a saint by the Ethiopian Orthodox Tewahedo Church.

Lalibela's life was recorded in the Gadla Lalibela, a hagiographic text. He was born in 1162 AD in the town of Roha, later renamed Lalibela in his honor. According to tradition, a swarm of bees surrounded him at birth and his mother interpreted it as a symbol of future greatness. He was given the name "Lalibela," meaning "the bees recognize his royalty" in Old Agaw.

This prophecy marked Lalibela for greatness, but it also sparked conflict and jealousy, forcing him to flee to Jerusalem, where he remained for several years. After returning to Ethiopia, he married Meskel Kibra. However, due to continued unrest in Lasta, the couple went into exile once again.

During this period, Lalibela had a dream which inspired him to build a "New Jerusalem" in Ethiopia. This vision came in response to the fall of the original Jerusalem to Muslim forces under Saladin in 1187 AD. He named the town Lalibela and called the river running through it the River Jordan (Amharic: ዮርዳኖስ ወንዝ).

Today, Lalibela remains renowned for its rock-hewn churches and once served as Ethiopia's capital.

ETHIOPIAN EMPIRE

PRESIDENT NELSON MANDELA

Nelson Mandela was a freedom fighter and the first Black President of South Africa from 1994 to 1999, formerly part of the Xhosa Kingdom known as Thembuland.

King Sarhili, a Xhosa monarch, resisted British colonial expansion but was ultimately defeated during the colonial conflicts. Nelson Mandela (Xhosa: [xolíɬaɬa mandêːla]), born Rolihlahla Mandela on July 18, 1918, in Mvezo, South Africa, was a Xhosa-speaking member of the Thembu royal family who rose to become one of the most influential leaders in the fight against apartheid. In response to the establishment of apartheid by the National Party, a system of institutionalized racial segregation, Mandela and the ANC dedicated themselves to ending white minority rule.

After studying law at the University of Fort Hare and the University of the Witwatersrand, he began his legal career in Johannesburg, where he became active in anti-colonial politics, joined the African National Congress (ANC) in 1943, and co-founded its Youth League in 1944.

As president of the ANC's Transvaal branch, Mandela played key roles in campaigns in the 1952 Defiance Campaign and 1955 Congress of the People. Although initially committed to nonviolent protest, Mandela's views evolved. Influenced by Marxist ideas, he secretly joined the banned South African Communist Party (SACP) and, in 1961, co-founded uMkhonto eSizwe, the armed wing of the ANC that led a campaign against the apartheid regime. Mandela was arrested in 1962 and remained imprisoned for 27 years. In

1990, amid rising domestic unrest and mounting international pressure, President F. W. de Klerk ordered his release.

Together, they led negotiations that brought an end to apartheid, culminating in South Africa's first multiracial democratic elections in 1994. Mandela was elected president and led a government of national unity, dedicated to healing the country's deep racial divisions. His administration focused on reconciliation, nation-building, and economic reform. He established the Truth and Reconciliation Commission to address past human rights abuses and promoted policies aimed at reducing poverty and expanding healthcare. After his presidency, he continued his advocacy through the Nelson Mandela Foundation, focusing on issues such as HIV/AIDS and poverty.

Mandela became a global symbol of democracy, justice, and peace. He received more than 250 honors, including the Nobel Peace Prize. Revered both in South Africa and around the world, he is known by his Thembu clan name, Madiba, and is often referred to as the "Father of the Nation."

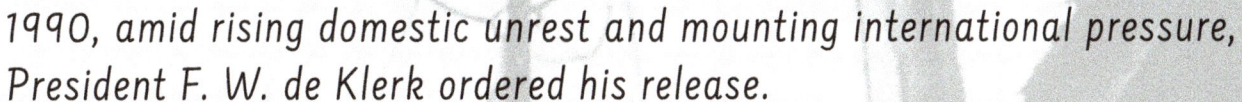

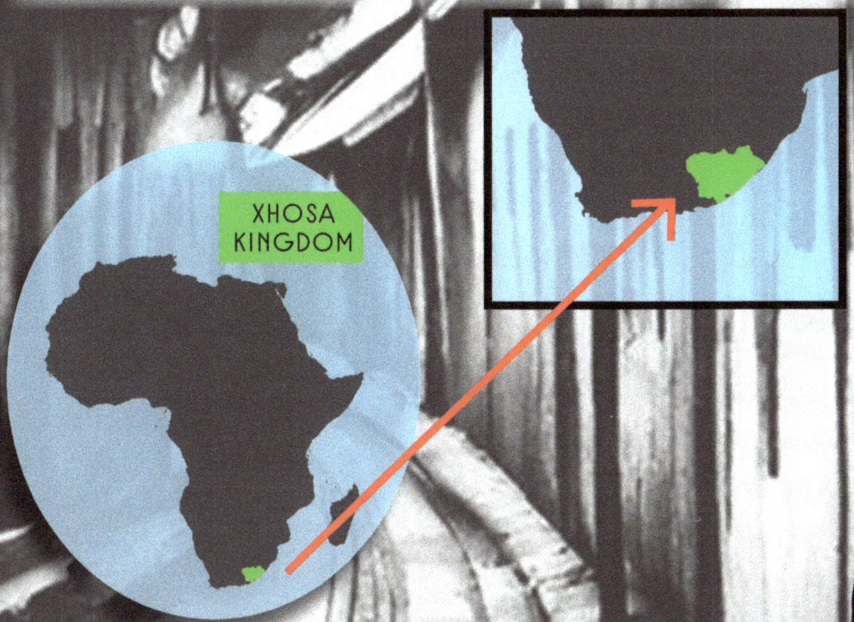

MANSA MUSA

Mansa Musa was the ninth Mansa of the Mali Empire from 1312 AD to 1337 AD, now modern-day Mali. Musa remains one of the richest people in history—even to this day!

Mansa Musa was a powerful king in West Africa. Mansa" translates to "king" or "ruler" in the Mandé language, which is why he was called Mansa Musa, meaning "King Musa." His name, Musa (Arabic: موسى), means the same as prophet Moses in Islamic tradition. Oral traditions and historical texts like the Timbuktu Chronicles also refer to him as Kanku Musa, meaning "Musa, son of Kanku," reflecting the Mandé custom of naming children after their mothers.

According to Musa, his predecessor launched two expeditions to explore the Atlantic Ocean. The first with 200 ships, and the second, led by the emperor himself, with 2,000 ships. Musa was left to rule during the second voyage and became emperor

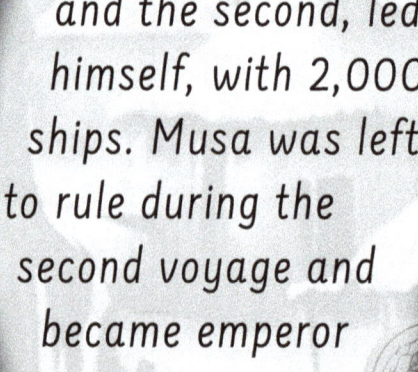

MALI EMPIRE

when his predecessor did not return.

His empire, Mali, became very wealthy by trading salt from the north and gold from the south from the rich mining regions of Bambuk and Bure. Over time, his empire accumulated vast amounts of gold. Mali was a major trading hub for goods such as ivory, slaves, spices, silks, and ceramics as well.

In 1324 BCE, Musa went on a very special trip called a Hajj, a pilgrimage to the holy city of Mecca. He brought thousands of people with him, along with camels carrying loads of gold. Everywhere he went, people were amazed by his riches and kindness. His journey helped make Mali famous around the world.

Musa expanded the Mali Empire to include important cities like Gao and Timbuktu. During his pilgrimage to Mecca, he conquered 24 cities and brought back skilled architects from Cairo, Egypt, and Andalusia, Spain. With their help, he built a grand palace in Timbuktu and the famous Djinguereber Mosque, which still stands today.

Mansa Musa's legacy lives on through the Djinguereber Mosque, the University of Sankore, and his enduring influence on West African history and Islamic culture. Under his rule, the University of Sankore thrived, with specialists teaching subjects like law, astronomy, and mathematics. Musa turned Timbuktu into a center of learning and culture by attracting scholars, poets, and legal experts from across the world.

ASKIA MUHAMMAD

Askia Muhammad Ture was ruler of the Askia Dynasty of the Songhai Empire from 1493 AD to 1528 AD, now modern-day Mali. Muhammad was known as "Askia the Great."

In 1493 AD, Muhammad rose to power and made political, economic, and cultural reforms. Muhammad expanded the Songhai Empire, making it the largest in West African history.

He standardized trade measures, regulated commerce, secured trade routes, and implemented an organized tax system, all of which strengthened the empire's economic foundation.

Muhammad divided the empire into provinces, each overseen by centrally appointed governors. Also, he established ministries for agriculture, finance, internal affairs, and justice. He allied with scholars of Timbuktu to produce African and Islamic historical texts.

Muhammad's legacy endures through his burial site, the Tomb of Askia, which is now a UNESCO World Heritage Site.

EMPEROR MENELIK I

Emperor Menelik I was an Emperor of the Solomonic Dynasty of the Ethiopian Empire, now modern-day Ethiopia. According to one Ethiopian tradition, he was born in Mai-Bela, near the village of Addi-Shmagle, northwest of present-day Asmara in Eritrea. Menelik, the son of King Solomon and the Queen of Sheba, was called "son of the wise."

King Solomon sent Israelites with Menelik (Ge'ez: ምኒልክ, Mənilək), to rule according to biblical principles. Some traditions say that Solomon gave Menelik the Ark of the Covenant, while others claim that Menelik and his Israelite companions took it with them when they left. Solomon attempted to reclaim the Ark but was unable to do so, as its supernatural properties protected Menelik. However, after his mother's death, Menelik was crowned King of Ethiopia.

Menelik, an emperor of Ethiopia's Solomonic dynasty, claimed descent from King Solomon. The dynasty ruled the country for nearly 3,000 years, ending in 1974 with the reign of its last monarch, Emperor Haile Selassie.

After his death, Menelik's remains were gathered by the clergy of Axum and placed in the Cathedral of St. Mary of Zion in Axum.

KING NARMER

King Narmer was the first King of the First Dynasty of Ancient Egypt from c. 3050 BCE, now modern-day Egypt. Narmer founded the first centralized state in Ancient Egypt by unifying Upper and Lower Egypt, laying the foundation for one of the world's oldest civilizations.

Narmer succeeded King Ka and was the first pharaoh to rule over a united kingdom. The name "Narmer" meaning "fierce catfish" or "stinging catfish," was his Horus name, a title used by Egyptian kings, while "Menes" is believed to have been his birth name. New Kingdom king lists identify Menes as the first human ruler of Egypt.

Neithhotep was the wife of Narmer and the mother of his successor, Hor-Aha. Also, Neithhotep may have ruled as pharaoh in her own right, which would make her the earliest known female monarch in recorded history.

The Narmer Palette, a ceremonial artifact, depicts Narmer wearing the White Crown of Upper Egypt on one side and the Red Crown of Lower Egypt on the other, symbolizing his unification of the Two Lands.

ANCIENT EGYPT

KING PIYE

King Piye was the first King of the Kushite Kingdom of Nubia and founder of the Twenty-fifth Dynasty of Ancient Egypt from 744 BCE to 714 BCE, now modern-day Sudan and Egypt, respectively.

Piye ruled both Nubia and Upper Egypt from the city of Napata, a major political and religious center of the Kushite Kingdom located in present-day Sudan. During his reign, Piye adopted two throne names Usimare and Sneferre. In a military campaign to reunify Egypt, he led his army northward and stopped in Thebes to take part in the Opet Festival, a significant religious celebration that reinforced his authority over Upper Egypt. Viewing the campaign as a holy war, Piye instructed his soldiers to purify themselves and offer sacrifices to the god Amun before going into battle. After securing victory, he returned south, first to Thebes and then to his capital in Nubia.

As a follower of the god Amun, Piye restored Egypt's religious traditions. He hired skilled Egyptian sculptors and stonemasons to rebuild the Great Temple of Amun at Jebel Barkal, a sacred site originally constructed by Pharaoh Thutmose III.

By the end of his reign, Piye had firmly established Kushite power in Egypt and laid the foundation for a line of Nubian kings who would rule for nearly a century. This era, known as the "Black Pharaohs," marked a powerful chapter in both Egyptian and Nubian history.

KING QA'A

King Qa'a was the last King of the First Dynasty of Ancient Egypt from 2033 BCE to 2001 BCE, now modern-day Egypt. His name, Qa'a, means 'His arm is raised.'

Several stone vessel inscriptions mention that Qa'a celebrated his first Sed festival, a major royal jubilee traditionally held in the 30th year of a king's reign. Since Sed festivals were held every three years after the first jubilee, a second Sed festival was celebrated during Qa'a's reign, indicating he ruled for at least 33 years.

On the Abydos King List, Qebeh, Qa'a's cartouche and Sextus Julius Africanus, recorded Qa'a reigned for 33 years.

The Palermo Stone, a significant histaorical record from ancient Egypt, confirmed Qa'a's coronation year and cultic ceremonies during his reign.

Additionally, numerous ivory tags dating to Qa'a's time have been discovered. These tags typically describe standard royal activities, such as the cataloging of burial offerings and inventories of the king's personal possessions.

PTAH

Ptah was known as God in Ancient Egypt, around 3000 BCE, now modern-day Egypt. Ptah conceived the world in his heart and brought it into existence through the power of speech.

The Shabaka Stone, from the Twenty-Fifth Dynasty, recorded Ptah 'gave life to all the gods and their kas through his heart and his tongue.' In the Memphite Triad, he was the husband of the goddess Sekhmet and the father of Imhotep and Nefertem. The Memphite religion believed in creation through divine thought and the power of the spoken word. A hymn to Ptah from the Twenty-second Dynasty, said Ptah "crafted the world in the design of his heart." Ptah was a god who listened to prayers. Ptah (Ancient Egyptian: pth) was a creator god and the protector of craftsmen and architects. The ancient city of Memphis was dedicated to his worship and protection. At Memphis, large ears were carved into temple walls to symbolize his role as the god who hears and responds to the prayers of his followers. Near Deir el-Medina, a special oratory was built in his honor.

The great temple, Hut-ka-Ptah meaning 'Enclosure of the ka of Ptah' was one of the city's most prominent structures. The name Hut-ka-Ptah influenced the Ancient Greek word Aiguptos (Αἴγυπτος), which became Aegyptus in Latin, later evolving into Egypte in Middle French, and eventually into the English word "Egypt."

The American city of Memphis, Tennessee, shares its name with the Ancient Egyptian capital. The name was chosen to reflect a connection between the two cities, both located

ANCIENT EGYPT

near significant rivers, the Mississippi and the Nile, and to evoke the cultural grandeur of Ancient Egypt.

Ptah had many roles in Ancient Egyptian religion and in society:
- Ptah the begetter of the first beginning
- Ptah lord of truth
- Ptah lord of eternity
- Ptah who listens to prayers
- Ptah master of ceremonies
- Ptah master of justice
- Ptah the God who made himself to be God
- Ptah the double being
- Ptah the beautiful face

Ptah was mummified as a man with green skin, symbolizing rebirth and regeneration. He wore a tight-fitting shroud and a false beard, and held a staff that combined three powerful symbols:

Sceptre – representing power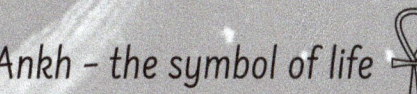

Ankh – the symbol of life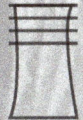

Djed Pillar – representing stability

These three combined symbols were the three creative powers of the God of Creation: power (was), life (ankh) and stability (djed).

PHARAOH RAMESSES II

Pharaoh Ramesses II was the third Pharaoh of the Nineteenth Dynasty of Ancient Egypt from 1279 BCE to 1213 BCE during the New Kingdom period, now modern-day Egypt. Ramesses II was the greatest, most celebrated, and most powerful pharaoh.

Ramesses II was not born a prince but rose to greatness as the grandson of Ramesses I, whose name means "Ra bore him." Ramesses I focused on domestic affairs and completed the second pylon at Karnak Temple, a project initiated under Horemheb, the last Pharaoh of the 18th Dynasty. This work helped bridge the transition between Horemheb's stabilizing reign and the powerful rule of his son, Seti I. After Ramesses I death, Seti I became king, and his son Ramesses II was named crown prince at age fourteen. Ramesses II became Pharaoh on 31 May 1279 BCE.

Ramesses II was Egypt's most successful warrior. He led at least 15 military wars and had an army of 100,000 men. In the north, he fought to reclaim territories in Canaan and Phoenicia, restoring Egyptian control. Although Nubia had been established for two centuries, Ramesses II led military campaigns in the south and reinforced Egyptian dominance by constructing the temples of Beit el-Wali and Gerf Hussein.

Ramesses II defeated the Sherden sea pirates, who had attacked Egypt's Mediterranean trade routes. By setting strategic traps along the coast, he launched a surprise naval assault and captured them all. A stele from Tanis recorded that "none were able to stand before them."

Ramesses II was a prolific builder. He moved the capital from Thebes to Pi-Ramesses in the eastern Nile Delta. This new city, Pi-Ramesses Aa-nakhtu means "Domain of Ramesses, Great in Victory", featured vast temples, storerooms, a royal palace, and even a zoo. Archaeological remains include mudbrick granaries and a scribe school.

He also built the Ramesseum in Thebes and the magnificent temple complex at Abu Simbel. In 1255 BCE, Ramesses II and Queen Nefertari traveled to Nubia, where Abu Simbel was carved into the rock. The temple symbolized Ramesses' divine power of his "ego cast in stone." His temple complex was the most elaborate since the pyramids, nearly 1,500 years earlier. Ramesses II was the Pharaoh mentioned in the Biblical Book of Exodus (Genesis 47:11; Exodus 1:11).

Ramesses II was worshipped during his lifetime and honored as the "Great Ancestor" by later pharaohs. He celebrated thirteen Sed festivals, lived to around 90 years old, and was buried in the Valley of the Kings. Ramesses II appeared in films such as 'The Prince of Egypt' (1998) and 'Exodus: Gods and Kings' (2014). His mummy, later relocated to the Royal Cache, is now on display at the National Museum of Egyptian Civilization in Cairo, Egypt.

ANCIENT EGYPT

EMPEROR SEPTIMIUS SEVERUS

Emperor Septimius Severus was the Emperor and Founder of the Severan Dynasty of the Roman Empire, from 193 AD to 211 AD, later called Rome, now modern-day Italy. Severus' shift toward a militarized form of governance, restored order and eliminated corruption.

Septimus Severus was born in Leptis Magna, in the Roman province of Africa, now modern-day Al-Khums, Libya. Severus rose to power during the Roman empire's most turbulent periods. In 197 AD, Severus expanded the Roman army by increasing troop numbers and stationed soldiers near the capital. This created a strategic reserve force capable of rapid deployment throughout the empire. To secure the loyalty of his troops, he granted each soldier a bonus of 250 denarii and raised annual pay from 300 to 400 denarii.

Severus was the final contender to emerge victorious during the Year of the Five Emperors in 193 AD, following the death of Emperor Pertinax. After consolidating power in the western provinces, he launched a successful campaign against the Parthian Empire, capturing Ctesiphon in 197 AD and pushing the eastern frontier to the Tigris River.

In 202 AD, he campaigned in Mauritania against the Garamantes, capturing their capital Garama and extending the Limes

Tripolitanus, a defensive network of forts and roads, to secure the southern desert frontier. He invested in agricultural development, ensuring the stability and food supply of the empire.

Severus contributed significantly to architecture and urban development. In Rome, he commissioned the Septizodium, an ornate monumental façade. During his visit to Leptis Magna in 203 AD, he oversaw major public works, including a triumphal arch that symbolized the integration of provincial cities into Roman identity. In 208 AD, Severus led a campaign to Britain, reinforcing Hadrian's Wall and reoccupying the Antonine Wall. He invaded Caledonia, now modern-day Scotland, with a force of 50,000 men, to capture the northern tribes.

After his military victories in the East, Severus commemorated his achievements by building the Arch of Septimius Severus in the Roman Forum, a lasting symbol of his power and legacy as a conqueror.

PHARAOH NEFERKARE SHABAKA

Pharaoh Neferkare Shabaka was the third Pharaoh of the Kushite Kingdom in Nubia from 722 BCE to 707 BCE, now modern-day Sudan.

Shabaka (Meroitic: 935 𓃭𓃭𓃭 sha-ba-ka; Egyptian: 𓈙𓃀𓎡 š₃ b₃ k₃) controlled all of Egypt. He established his royal seat at Thebes and built a pink granite statue of himself at Karnak, where he wore the double crown of Upper and Lower Egypt, symbolizing his unified rule. He made Memphis, near modern-day Cairo, Egypt, the capital and constructed numerous religious buildings at Thebes, the spiritual center and home of Amun-Re. Shabaka successfully preserved Egypt's independence from the Neo-Assyrian Empire under Sargon II. He showed appreciation for Egypt's ancient traditions in the art and architecture of his reign.

One of the most important artifacts from his reign was the Shabaka Stone, which recorded a collection of religious and philosophical texts originally dating back to the Old Kingdom. These texts were inscribed to protect and preserve Egypt's ancient heritage. Also, the Shabaka Gate, a stone doorway, once guarded the royal treasury chambers.

Shabaka was buried at el-Kurru, the royal cemetery of the Kushite Kings. A sphinx head representing Shabaka, now housed at the Egyptian Museum in Cairo, blends Nubian and Egyptian artistic styles, symbolizing his heritage and role in revitalizing Egypt's cultural legacy.

KING SHAKA ZULU

King Shaka Zulu was King of the Zulu Kingdom from 1816 to 1828, now modern-day South Africa. Shaka was one of the most influential leaders in African history for revolutionizing the military and political systems.

Shaka was born in the lunar month of uNtulikazi (July) in 1787 AD, in the region of Mthonjaneni, now modern-day KwaZulu-Natal, South Africa. Shaka transformed the Zulu military into one of the most formidable forces in southern Africa. He introduced the iklwa, a short stabbing spear ideal for close combat, replacing the traditional throwing spear. He redesigned the Nguni shield to be larger and more durable, allowing warriors to use it both defensively and offensively.

His most famous battlefield innovation was the "bull horn" formation:

- The Chest (umkhonto): Veteran warriors engaged the enemy frontally.
- The Horns (izimpondo): Younger warriors flanked the enemy from both sides.
- The Loins (umava): A reserve force, kept calm and ready, reinforced weak points or delivered the final blow.

Shaka implemented an age-grade regimental system, grouping young men into age-based units subjected to strict discipline and intense training. Warriors endured long marches of up to 80 kilometers (50 miles) a day without footwear to harden them. Boys as young as six began service as udibi, apprentice warriors who carried supplies, gradually integrating into combat roles.

Key victories at Gqokli Hill (1818) and the Battle of the Mhlatuze River solidified Zulu dominance by defeating the powerful Ndwandwe under Zwide.

Shaka's legacy extends beyond the battlefield. King Shaka International Airport (opened in 2010) and uShaka Marine World in Durban are modern tributes to his enduring influence. A statue of Shaka also stands in Camden Market, London.

Shaka Zulu remains a symbol of African resilience, military innovation, and nation-building, whose legacy still resonates today.

KING SOLOMON

King Solomon was the fourth King of the Kingdom of Israel and Judah from 970 BCE to 931 BCE, now modern-day Israel. Solomon was the ruler of Twelve Tribes and son of David and Bathsheba. Solomon was a legendary figure of wisdom, wealth, and political power.

Solomon built the First Temple in Jerusalem, which became the spiritual center of Israelite worship. His reign was known as the "Golden Age" of ancient Israel which lasted 40 years (1 Kings 11:42). Solomon's rule was marked by peace, prosperity, cultural achievements, and diplomacy. According to biblical tradition, Solomon was a prolific writer and composed these three biblical books:

- Proverbs (Mishlei) - A collection of moral and practical wisdom.
- Ecclesiastes (Kohelet) - A philosophical reflection on the meaning of life.
- Song of Songs (Shir HaShirim) - A poetic and symbolic exploration of love, interpreted both romantically and spiritually Psalms 72 and 127.

Solomon's wisdom and reputation attracted international attention. The Queen of Sheba traveled to Jerusalem and was impressed by his wisdom and generosity. She returned home with gifts (1 Kings 10:1-13 and 2 Chronicles 9:1-12). According to Ethiopian tradition,

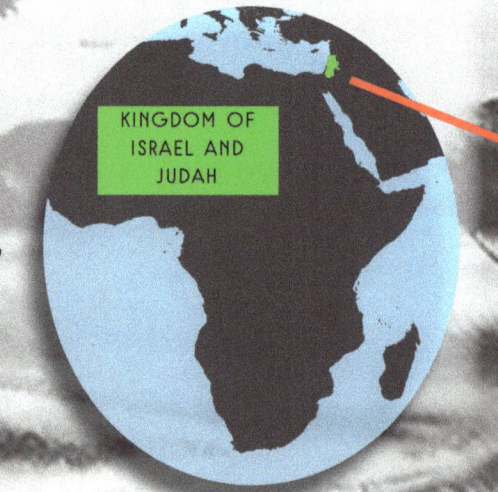

preserved in the Kebra Nagast, the Queen of Sheba had a son by Solomon, who gave birth beside the Mai Bella stream in the province of Hamasien, Eritrea, named Menelik I, King of Axum. He later became the first emperor of Ethiopia and founded the Solomonic Dynasty, that would reign as Jewish, then Christian, Empire of Ethiopia which lasted 3000 years, until Haile Selassie in 1974 AD.

This tradition claims Solomon gave Menelik a replica of the Ark of the Covenant, while the original was secretly brought to Axum, Ethiopia. Ethiopian Christians continue to believe that the true Ark remains hidden there in the Church of Our Lady Mary of Zion, guarded by a single priest.

The Qur'an presents him as a righteous ruler with the ability to communicate with animals and command supernatural beings. Over time, non-biblical traditions portrayed Solomon as a magician and with his name in magical texts.

Solomon is revered in Judaism and Christianity for his wisdom, and in Islam as a prophet.

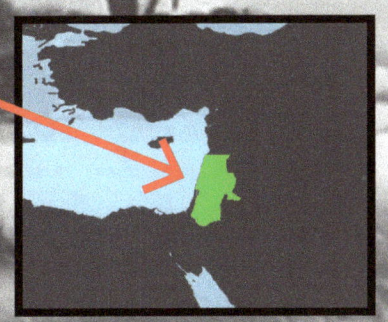

PHARAOH TAHARQA

Pharaoh Taharqa was King of the Kushite Kingdom in Nubia and Pharaoh of the Twenty-fifth Dynasty of Ancient Egypt, from 690 BCE to 664 BCE, now modern-day Sudan and Egypt, respectively. Taharqa helped preserve Egypt's autonomy and elevated Nubia.

He was the son of King Piye, the Kushite King of Nubia who first conquered Ancient Egypt. Taharqa inherited a powerful empire stretching from modern-day Sudan to the Nile Delta and ruled over Ancient Egypt for 100 years.

Ancient Egypt and Kush experienced prosperity, marked by high Nile floods, abundant harvests, and administrative stability. Taharqa's reign blended Kushite traditions with Egyptian culture, reinforcing a Nubian-Egyptian identity. His era is noted for religious reform, architectural grandeur, and foreign policy.

Taharqa was a devout follower of Amun and invested heavily in temple construction. He donated vast amounts of gold to the temple at Kawa and restored and commissioned major temples at Karnak, Jebel Barkal, and Kawa. Jebel Barkal became a monumental religious center modeled after Karnak, serving both spiritual and administrative functions. These temple towns functioned as centers of local governance and redistribution, illustrating how religious architecture served statecraft.

Taharqa also revived pyramid construction in Nubia, the first large-scale pyramid building since Egypt's Middle Kingdom. His pyramid at Nuri, near El-Kurru, is the largest in Nubia, with a base of over 50 meters. His elaborate burial included more than 1,070 shabtis, made from granite, ankerite, and alabaster.

On the international stage, Taharqa pursued alliances in Phoenicia and Philistia to counter Assyrian expansion. He maintained a strong military and personally trained in long-distance running to uphold physical readiness, a Kushite tradition. He is "Tirhakah" (הָקְהָרְת) in the Hebrew Bible (2 Kings 19:9, Isaiah 37:9), where he appears as a Kushite king who came to aid Hezekiah of Judah during the Assyrian siege of Jerusalem in 701 BCE.

Taharqa's reign left a lasting legacy of cultural fusion, architectural achievement, and resistance to foreign domination.

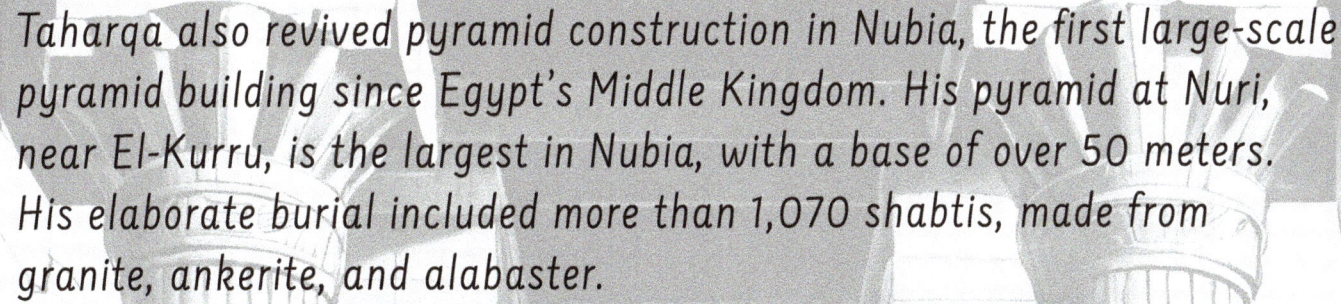

KABAKA TTEMBO

Kabaka Ttembo was the fourth Kabaka of the Kingdom of Buganda from 1404 AD to 1434 AD, last called Buganda, now modern-day Uganda.

Kabaka means "king" and Ttembo was the son of King Kimera and his mother was Nattembo.

Ttembo came to power however, the truth of the story remains uncertain. According to oral tradition, during a hunting trip with his grandfather, Ttembo struck him on the head with a club, resulting in his grandfather's death.

Ttembo chose Ntinda Hill as his royal residence and administrative center. The hill became the seat of his authority and holds historical significance in the early political development of Buganda.

KING TUTANKHAMUN

King Tutankhamun was a Pharaoh of the Eighteenth Dynasty of Ancient Egypt from 1332 BCE to 1323 BCE, now modern-day Egypt. Tutankhamun was known as "Boy King" and restorer of ancient traditions.

Tutankhamun, originally named Tutankhaten, was born around 1341 BCE during a time of great religious change in ancient Egypt. His father, Pharaoh Akhenaten, had introduced a new religion centered on the sun god Aten, abandoning the long-standing worship of multiple gods. His mother is believed to have been Akhenaten's sister, Younger Lady, which was a common practice in royal families to preserve the bloodline.

Tutankhamun became pharaoh at just nine years old, earning him the title "Boy King." Early in his reign, he began to distance himself from his father's religious revolution. With guidance from powerful advisers like Ay and Horemheb, he restored Egypt's religion back to the worship of Amun, and changed his name from Tutankhaten to Tutankhamun, meaning "Living Image of Amun."

He moved the royal court from Amarna, Akhenaten's capital, back to Memphis, a former political and religious center. Amun regained its religious festivals, temples, and priesthoods were reinstated. These efforts were documented in the Restoration Stela, which celebrated his commitment to reviving the old ways.

Tutankhamun re-established ties with Mitanni, and directed military activity in Nubia and the Near East. He was one of the few pharaohs to be worshipped as a god during his lifetime. Despite his young age, he constructed a royal tomb and mortuary temple, though both remained unfinished due to his unexpected death at around 18 years old.

Today, Tutankhamun is one of the most famous pharaohs of all time, known for his golden mask and the mystery of his short life.

KING USERKRAF

King Userkraf was King and Founder of the Fifth Dynasty of Ancient Egypt from 2492 BCE to 2487 BCE, now modern-day Egypt. Userkraf was the sun king of Egypt's Old Kingdom.

He served as a high priest of Ra, the powerful sun god. His reign marked a turning point in Egyptian religion, art, and foreign engagement.

Userkaf solar worshiped more than any pharaoh before him. He was the first king to build a sun temple, the Nekhenre ("Stronghold of Ra"), located between Abusir and Abu Gurab, Egypt. This temple was not only a place of worship but also a symbol of the king's divine connection to Ra. It hosted rituals honoring the setting sun, which Egyptians believed represented both the end of life and the promise of rebirth. Userkaf established himself as the "Son of Ra," chosen to rule.

The Royal Annals of the Old Kingdom record offerings of bread, beer, and land to various temples. One notable contribution was to the Temple of Montu, the war god, at El-Tod in Upper Egypt.
His reign marked early Egyptian foreign contact. Carvings at his mortuary complex in Saqqara show ships on long voyages, trading with lands across the Aegean Sea. A stone vase bearing the name of Userkaf's sun temple was discovered on the Greek island of Kythira,

and early cross-cultural exchanges.

Userkaf's legacy continues with a painted limestone head of the king wearing the Hedjet (White Crown of Upper Egypt) preserved in the Cleveland Museum of Art. Additionally, a massive sphinx head from his mortuary temple was uncovered and now housed in the Egyptian Museum in Cairo. His innovations in religion, trade, and royal symbolism helped shape Egyptian civilization for generations.

HIS LEGACY CONTINUES...

"Wisdom builds legacy; understanding preserves it."
~ King Solomon

ABOUT THE AUTHOR

My name is Kristan Hypolite, M. Ed. I am the proud father of Kaleb Hypolite, an enthusiastic educator, and an entrepreneur.

As a father, I am amazed by Kaleb's brilliant and witty personality. We keep our mind sharp by playing chess, checkers, and puzzles. We stay active by playing basketball, flag football, and soccer.

In addition to sports and recreation, we have a keen interest in traveling, world history and music, especially Afro beats, reggae, and soca. We find these activities not only bring us joy but help us relax and unwind.

As an educator with a Masters Degree in Special Education, I am committed to providing a nurturing and inclusive learning environment for all future kings and queens. I believe they are capable of achieving greatness with the proper resources and supports.

As an entrepreneur, I'm dedicated to teaching principles and providing access to resources for all kings and queens to establish generational wealth.

ABOUT THE BOOK

African Kings uncovers the epic stories of powerful leaders who ruled empires, commanded armies, and shaped the course of civilizations. From the legendary wealth of Mansa Musa of Mali to the divine wisdom of King Solomon of Israel, the youthful brilliance of King Tutankhamun of Egypt, and the fierce military genius of Shaka Zulu of South Africa, this book celebrates extraordinary men whose legacies still echo through history.

Discover how Shaka Zulu revolutionized warfare with unstoppable tactics. Explore Mansa Musa's golden pilgrimage that dazzled the world. Experience the restoration of a fractured kingdom under the youthful brilliance of Tutankhamun. Journey through the ancient courts of Solomon, where wisdom reigned with unmatched clarity and vision.

Whether forging alliances, leading warriors into battle, or commanding respect through sheer charisma, these men stood as enduring symbols of leadership, strength, and resilience. These kings were more than rulers, they were strategists, builders, diplomats, and warriors. They faced impossible odds, defended their lands, united their people, and ruled with both might and purpose.

African Kings is more than a historical account, it's a celebration of greatness. Their courage still resonates today, reminding us that true power lies not just in the throne, but in the legacy one leaves behind. Their stories continue to inspire, proving that greatness is timeless and leadership lives on through the generations.

REFERENCES

1. African American Registry. (n.d.). African voyage to the Americas: A story. https://aaregistry.org/story/african-voyage-to-the-americas-a-story/
2. AfroLegends. (2012, May 14). Béhanzin: One of the last African resistors to colonization. https://afrolegends.com/2012/05/14/sans-parole-sans-honneur-la-loi-du-materialisme-behanzin-one-of-the-last-african-resistant-to-colonization/
3. Ancient Egypt Online. (n.d.). Biography of Userkaf. https://www.ancient-egypt.org/history/old-kingdom/5th-dynasty/userkaf/biography-of-userkaf.html
4. Archaeological Museum at Johns Hopkins University. (n.d.). Ptah: Ancient Egyptian amulets. https://archaeologicalmuseum.jhu.edu/staff-projects/ancient-egyptian-amulets/ptah/
5. BBC. (2019, February 26). Nelson Mandela: Life and legacy. https://www.bbc.com/news/world-africa-47379458
6. BBC History. (n.d.). Imhotep. https://www.bbc.co.uk/history/historic_figures/imhotep.shtml
7. Cleveland Museum of Art. (n.d.). Painted limestone head of King Userkaf. [Museum object].
8. Education National Geographic. (n.d.). Haile Selassie becomes emperor of Ethiopia. https://education.nationalgeographic.org/resource/haile-selassie-becomes-emperor-ethiopia/
9. Encyclopædia Britannica. (n.d.). Akhenaten. https://www.britannica.com/biography/Akhenaten
10. Encyclopædia Britannica. (n.d.). Benin: History. https://www.britannica.

com/place/Benin/History
11. Encyclopædia Britannica. (n.d.). Haile Selassie. https://www.britannica.com/biography/Haile-Selassie
12. Encyclopædia Britannica. (n.d.). Hannibal. https://www.britannica.com/biography/Hannibal-Carthaginian-general-247-183-BCE
13. Encyclopædia Britannica. (n.d.). Imhotep. https://www.britannica.com/biography/Imhotep
14. Encyclopædia Britannica. (n.d.). Khufu. https://www.ebsco.com/research-starters/history/khufu
15. Encyclopædia Britannica. (n.d.). Menilek I. https://www.britannica.com/biography/Menilek-I
16. Encyclopædia Britannica. (n.d.). Muhammad I Askia. https://www.britannica.com/biography/Muhammad-I-Askia
17. Encyclopædia Britannica. (n.d.). Nelson Mandela. https://www.britannica.com/biography/Nelson-Mandela
18. Encyclopædia Britannica. (n.d.). Ramesses II. https://www.britannica.com/biography/Ramses-II-king-of-Egypt
19. Encyclopædia Britannica. (n.d.). Septimius Severus. https://www.britannica.com/biography/Septimius-Severus
20. Encyclopædia Britannica. (n.d.). Shabaka. https://www.britannica.com/biography/Shabaka
21. Encyclopædia Britannica. (n.d.). Solomon. https://www.britannica.com/biography/Solomon
22. Encyclopædia Britannica. (n.d.). Tutankhamun. https://www.britannica.com/biography/Tutankhamun

23. EBSCOhost. (n.d.). Kushite King Piye. https://www.ebsco.com/research-starters/history/kushite-king-piye
24. EBSCOhost. (n.d.). Taharqa. https://www.ebsco.com/research-starters/history/taharqa
25. English Heritage. (n.d.). Cetshwayo. https://www.english-heritage.org.uk/visit/blue-plaques/cetshwayo/
26. National Museum of Egyptian Civilization. (n.d.). Amenhotep I. https://nmec.gov.eg/mummies-hall/amenhotep-i/
27. Oxford Research Encyclopedia of African History. (n.d.). Imhotep. https://oxfordre.com/africanhistory/display/10.1093/acrefore/9780190277734.001.0001/acrefore-9780190277734-e-582
28. Panafrocore. (2024, June 20). King Kaleb of Axum (Saint Elesbaan): The remarkable king of Aksum. https://panafrocore.com/2024/06/20/king-kaleb-of-axum-saint-elesbaan-the-remarkable-king-of-aksum/
29. SA History Online. (n.d.). Shaka Zulu. https://www.sahistory.org.za/people/shaka-zulu
30. Wikipedia contributors. (n.d.). [Multiple biographies]. Wikipedia. https://en.wikipedia.org
31. (Include specific pages like: Akhenaten, Amenhotep I, Askia Muhammad I, Béhanzin, Cetshwayo, Djer, Endubis, Ghezo, Haile Selassie, Hannibal, Horemheb, Jaja of Opobo, Kaleb of Axum, Khufu, Lalibela, Mansa Musa, Menelik I, Narmer, Piye, Ptah, Qa'a, Ramesses II, Septimius Severus, Shabaka, Shaka, Solomon, Taharqa, Ttembo of Buganda, Tutankhamun, Userkaf, and the Atlantic voyage of the predecessor of Mansa Musa.)
32. World History Encyclopedia. (n.d.). Horemheb. https://www.worldhistory.org/Horemheb/
33. World History Encyclopedia. (n.d.). Narmer. https://www.worldhistory.org/Narmer/

34. World History EDU. (n.d.). Pharaoh Djer: History, reign & tomb. https://worldhistoryedu.com/pharaoh-djer-history-reign-tomb/
35. World History EDU. (n.d.). Ancient Egyptian Pharaoh Qa'a. https://worldhistoryedu.com/ancient-egyptian-pharaoh-qaa/
36.
37. References Links Draft
38. https://aaregistry.org/story/african-voyage-to-the-americas-a-story/
39. https://en.m.wikipedia.org/wiki/Atlantic_voyage_of_the_predecessor_of_Mansa_Musa
40. https://www.britannica.com/biography/Akhenaten/Religion-of-the-Aton
41. https://en.m.wikipedia.org/wiki/Akhenaten
42. https://nmec.gov.eg/mummies-hall/amenhotep-i/
43. https://en.m.wikipedia.org/wiki/Amenhotep_I
44. https://www.britannica.com/biography/Muhammad-I-Askia
45. https://en.m.wikipedia.org/wiki/Askia_Muhammad_I
46. https://en.m.wikipedia.org/wiki/B%C3%A9hanzin
47. https://afrolegends.com/2012/05/14/sans-parole-sans-honneur-la-loi-du-materialisme-behanzin-one-of-the-last-african-resistant-to-colonization/
48. https://en.m.wikipedia.org/wiki/Cetshwayo
49. https://www.english-heritage.org.uk/visit/blue-plaques/cetshwayo/#:~:text=THE%20RETURN%20TO%20ZULULAND&text=However%2C%20he%20was%20unable%20to,attack%2C%20though%20some%20suspected%20poisoning.
50. https://en.m.wikipedia.org/wiki/Djer
51. https://worldhistoryedu.com/pharaoh-djer-history-reign-tomb/
52. https://en.m.wikipedia.org/wiki/Endubis
53. https://en.m.wikipedia.org/wiki/Ghezo
54. https://www.britannica.com/place/Benin/History#ref517004

55. https://en.m.wikipedia.org/wiki/Haile_Selassie
56. https://education.nationalgeographic.org/resource/haile-selassie-becomes-emperor-ethiopia/
57. https://www.britannica.com/biography/Hannibal-Carthaginian-general-247-183-BCE
58. https://en.m.wikipedia.org/wiki/Hannibal
59. https://www.worldhistory.org/Horemheb/
60. https://en.m.wikipedia.org/wiki/Horemheb
61. https://www.britannica.com/biography/Imhotep
62. https://www.bbc.co.uk/history/historic_figures/imhotep.shtml
63. https://oxfordre.com/africanhistory/display/10.1093/acrefore/9780190277734.001.0001/acrefore-9780190277734-e-582
64. https://en.m.wikipedia.org/wiki/Jaja_of_Opobo
65. https://panafrocore.com/2024/06/20/king-kaleb-of-axum-saint-elesbaan-the-remarkable-king-of-aksum/
66. https://en.m.wikipedia.org/wiki/Kaleb_of_Axum
67. https://www.ebsco.com/research-starters/history/khufu
68. https://en.m.wikipedia.org/wiki/Khufu
69. https://www.jstor.org/stable/27026554
70. https://en.m.wikipedia.org/wiki/Gebre_Meskel_Lalibela
71. https://www.britannica.com/biography/Nelson-Mandela
72. https://en.m.wikipedia.org/wiki/Nelson_Mandela
73. https://www.bbc.com/news/world-africa-47379458
74. https://en.m.wikipedia.org/wiki/Mansa_Musa
75. https://en.m.wikipedia.org/wiki/Menelik_I
76. https://www.britannica.com/biography/Menilek-I
77. https://www.worldhistory.org/Narmer/
78. https://en.m.wikipedia.org/wiki/Narmer

79. https://www.ebsco.com/research-starters/history/kushite-king-piye#:~:text=Kushite%20King%20Piye%2C%20also%20known,of%20the%20Twenty%2DFifth%20Dynasty.
80. https://en.m.wikipedia.org/wiki/Piye
81. https://archaeologicalmuseum.jhu.edu/staff-projects/ancient-egyptian-amulets/ptah/
82. https://en.m.wikipedia.org/wiki/Ptah
83. https://worldhistoryedu.com/ancient-egyptian-pharaoh-qaa/
84. https://en.m.wikipedia.org/wiki/Qa%27a
85. https://www.britannica.com/biography/Ramses-II-king-of-Egypt
86. https://en.m.wikipedia.org/wiki/Ramesses_II
87. https://www.britannica.com/biography/Septimius-Severus
88. https://en.wikipedia.org/wiki/Septimius_Severus
89. https://www.britannica.com/biography/Shabaka
90. https://en.m.wikipedia.org/wiki/Shabaka
91. https://sahistory.org.za/people/shaka-zulu
92. https://en.m.wikipedia.org/wiki/Shaka
93. https://www.britannica.com/biography/Solomon
94. https://en.m.wikipedia.org/wiki/Solomon
95. https://www.ebsco.com/research-starters/history/taharqa
96. https://en.wikipedia.org/wiki/Taharqa
97. https://buganda.or.ug/
98. https://en.m.wikipedia.org/wiki/Ttembo_of_Buganda
99. https://www.britannica.com/biography/Tutankhamun
100. https://en.m.wikipedia.org/wiki/Tutankhamun
101. https://www.ancient-egypt.org/history/old-kingdom/5th-dynasty/userkaf/biography-of-userkaf.html
102. https://en.m.wikipedia.org/wiki/Userkaf

www.ingramcontent.com/pod-product-compliance
Lightning Source LLC
Chambersburg PA
CBHW051327110526
44582CB00003B/79